3496 8932

W9-BUY-042

# PUFFINS

A TRUE BOOK®

by

**Ann O. Squire**

**Children's Press®**
A Division of Scholastic Inc.

New York  Toronto  London  Auckland  Sydney
Mexico City  New Delhi  Hong Kong
Danbury, Connecticut

A boy in Iceland releasing a rescued Atlantic puffin chick

Content Consultant
**Kathy Carlstead, PhD**
Research Scientist
Honolulu Zoo

Reading Consultant
**Cecilia Minden-Cupp, PhD**
Former Director, Language and
Literacy Program
Harvard Graduate School
of Education

Author's Dedication
**For Isabel**

The photograph on the cover shows an Atlantic puffin. The photograph on the title page shows two Atlantic puffins in Greenland.

Library of Congress Cataloging-in-Publication Data
Squire, Ann.
   Puffins / by Ann O. Squire.
      p. cm. — (A True Book)
   Includes bibliographical references and index.
   ISBN-10:  0-516-25474-X (lib. bdg.)      0-516-25585-1 (pbk.)
   ISBN-13:  978-0-516-25474-6 (lib. bdg.)   978-0-516-25585-9 (pbk.)
   1. Puffins—Juvenile literature. I. Title. II. Series.
QL696.C42S68 2006
598.3'3—dc22                                      2005003637

CHILDREN'S PRESS, and A TRUE BOOK™, and associated logos are trademarks and/or registered trademarks of Scholastic Library Publishing. SCHOLASTIC and associated logos are trademarks and/or registered trademarks of Scholastic Inc.

1 2 3 4 5 6 7 8 9 10 R 16 15 14 13 12 11 10 09 08 07

# Contents

A colorful horned puffin stands on a cliff.

# A Colorful Bird

It takes just one look at a puffin's colorful beak and bright orange feet to see why this bird is called the clown of the ocean. Early sailors gave puffins the nickname "sea parrots." While they aren't parrots or clowns, puffins are certainly birds of the sea, or **seabirds**.

Puffins spend most of their lives in the open ocean. They depend on the ocean for food. They also need its rocky islands and shorelines to nest.

Most seabirds are good fliers, soaring through the air as they try to spot food in the ocean below. Puffins are much better swimmers than fliers, however. When a puffin wants to fly, it jumps off a cliff or moves along the

A puffin flies through the air (top) and swims in the ocean (bottom).

An Atlantic puffin flies along the water's surface before taking off.

water's surface until it gains enough speed to take off. Then it flaps its wings as fast as possible to keep its small, thick body in the air.

# A Puffin in the Air

A puffin can fly very fast in a straight line. It can travel 48 to 55 miles (77 to 89 kilometers) per hour. A rapid rate of flapping allows the puffin to fly so quickly. However, small wings keep the puffin from being able to change course easily in the air. That's why the puffin can't do quick takeoffs and makes hard landings. The penguin, another well-known seabird, cannot fly at all!

A puffin landing

When a puffin spots a fish, it dives underwater. Puffins use their wings to move through the water and their large, webbed feet to steer. Puffins zip easily through the water. It is hard to imagine that this bird cannot fly as well as it swims.

If you think about it, you'll realize that no bird can be good at both flying and swimming. Birds that are champion fliers need to be very light.

A tufted puffin looks for fish in the water.

Their bodies are small compared with their wings, and their bones are hollow.

A bird needs a very different kind of body to swim and dive underwater. A bird would pop to the surface like a cork if it had a light body. The best diving birds have heavy bodies and bones that help them stay underwater. Most diving birds have small wings. Large wings, necessary for flying, would just get in the way underwater. Even though a puffin is able to fly, its body is really designed for swimming.

A heavy body helps a puffin dive underwater.

# Puffins Everywhere

Puffins live throughout the Arctic. They can be found in both the Atlantic and the Pacific oceans. There are three kinds, or species, of puffins. The Atlantic puffin, once called the common puffin, lives in Iceland, Greenland, the British Isles, Nova Scotia, and Maine.

The Atlantic puffin is one of three kinds of puffins in the world.

The horned puffin (top) has a dark line, or "horn," that goes straight up above each eye. The tufted puffin (bottom) has a tuft of feathers behind each eye.

Two other puffin species, the horned puffin and the tufted puffin, live in the Pacific Ocean. These puffins can be found along the coasts of Siberia and Alaska. They may travel as far south as Oregon and California in the summer.

Puffin species have some differences. But all puffins have stocky bodies, sleek black feathers, and colorful feet and beaks. The puffin species are not all the same size. Horned puffins and Atlantic puffins stand about 12 inches (30 centimeters) high. Tufted puffins are a few inches taller, standing about 15 inches (38 cm) high.

The puffin's beak is one of its most unusual features. The puffin uses its beak as both a tool and a weapon.

When a puffin catches fish, it holds the **prey** in its beak with the heads hanging on one side and the tails on the other. The puffin opens its

An Atlantic puffin holds many fish in its beak.

beak and adds new fish to the ones already there. Puffins usually catch about ten fish during each dive. Some scientists have counted as many as sixty-four small fish in a puffin's beak.

How does the puffin manage to catch more fish without losing what's already in its mouth? The secret is spines on its tongue and on the roof of its mouth. These spines spear the tiny fish and

Spines on the tongue and the roof of the mouth help the puffin carry fish.

hold them so firmly that the puffin can open its mouth for more without the first ones falling out.

# Returning to Land

Puffins live out at sea in the winter. During that time, they cast off, or **molt**, their glossy black feathers. They also shed the top, colorful layer of their beak. The puffin's winter feathers and beak are drab and dull compared with their summer colors.

A group of Atlantic puffins gather at sea.

Everything changes as summer approaches. The puffin's beak and feet turn a vivid orange to prepare for the breeding season. Males have bigger and brighter beaks than females. The colorful beaks help the female puffins choose and identify mates.

The puffin begins the journey back to the island or shore where it was born. If this is the first year the puffin is breeding, it begins to look for a mate as

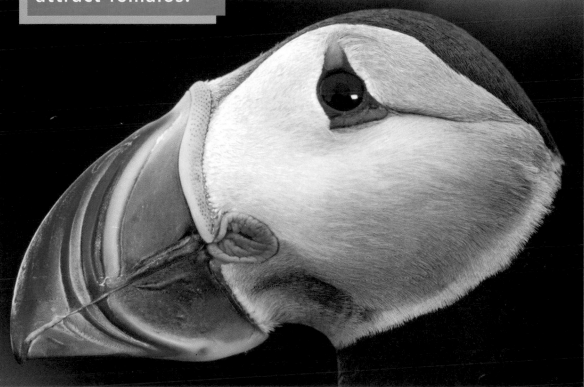

Male puffins have colorful beaks to attract females.

it gets close to land. If the puffin has raised a chick before, it looks around for its mate from last year.

Once the puffins have paired up, they prepare their nests. Puffins build nests in holes in the ground called **burrows**. The burrows are about 2 feet (60 cm) wide. The birds dig the burrow with their beaks. They kick the dirt out with their strong, webbed feet. Then they line the nest with grass and soft feathers. If the male and female find their burrow from the year before, they don't have to dig a new one.

A puffin stands in front of a burrow (top). Another puffin collects grass and soft feathers for the burrow's nest (bottom).

While they are working on the nest, the male and female puffins bow to each other, dance, and tap their bright beaks together. Then they mate.

Tufted puffins tap their beaks together.

A puffin egg lies in a nest.

Soon after, the female lays a single egg at the back of the burrow. Now she and her mate will **incubate** the egg by sitting on it and raise their chick together.

# A Puffling's Life

The egg hatches after the puffin pair takes turns incubating it for six to seven weeks. At first, the little puffin, called a **puffling**, cannot even keep itself warm. For the first week, one parent stands guard and warms the puffling while the other parent searches for food.

A new puffin chick needs its parents for warmth and food.

After the first week, the puffling is able to stay in the burrow alone. It still depends on its parents for food. They

must catch as many fish as
they can to feed their chick.
Puffin parents sometimes
make ten trips a day from
the ocean back to the burrow
with food for the fast-growing
puffling. When they return to
land, they drop their load of
fish near the opening of the
burrow so the little bird can
find it easily.

While it is young, the
puffling spends all its time in
the burrow. It never goes out

This puffling is one month old.

into the sunshine. The out-
doors is dangerous for puffin
chicks. Gulls and other
seabirds consider them a
tasty meal.

This full-grown puffin chick will leave the burrow soon.

After about eight weeks, it is time for the young puffin to leave the nest. The parents must return to the sea for the winter. The puffin begins to get hungry.

It waits until nighttime, when there are no gulls out hunting. Then the little puffin takes its first steps out of the nest. It finds its way to a cliff and jumps into the ocean far below.

The puffin will stay out at sea, traveling thousands of miles in search of food. Then one spring day, when the puffin is four or five years old, it will begin the long journey back home. It is time to find a mate and raise a chick of its own.

# Puffins and People

Although puffins are prey for gulls and other seabirds, their biggest dangers come from humans. People in the Arctic have hunted puffins for centuries. In the past, people used dogs to dig birds from their burrows. They also used long nets that look like lacrosse sticks to catch puffins.

A puffin catcher in Iceland snares a puffin with his net.

Humans ate puffin meat and eggs and made clothing out of the bird's tough skin.

In Maine, early settlers hunted and killed so many puffins that by 1900, the birds nearly disappeared. Fortunately, a con-servation program called Project Puffin tried using fake birds called **decoys** and other interesting methods to help puffins in Maine. The program successfully brought back groups, or **colonies**, of puffins to Maine.

A conservation program in Maine has helped bring back Atlantic puffins to the area.

One of the biggest threats to puffins today is **overfishing**. If people fish too much in certain areas, the puffins don't have enough to eat. Overfishing has been a disaster for a puffin colony on Rost Island in Norway. The Rost Island puffins could not find enough fish for their chicks in the past few years. Thousands of pufflings starved.

The search for oil also threatens puffins. Like penguins and other seabirds, puffins are vulnerable to oil spills and other pollution in the oceans. Tourism can be harmful, too. If visitors get too close, they

A puffin researcher measures an Atlantic puffin chick in Rost Island, Norway.

can frighten the puffin parents and cause them to leave their chicks.

People can protect puffins and other seabirds, however. We can reduce water pollution. We can work to prevent overfishing in ocean waters. And we can safeguard puffin lands. People can also help by supporting programs that work to bring breeding puffins back to areas where they once lived. By doing these things, we can create a world that is better for puffins and people alike.

Puffins return from sea to their nesting colony in Scotland.

# To Find Out More

Here are some additional resources to help you learn more about puffins:

 **Books**

Burnie, David. **Bird**. Dorling Kindersley Publishing, 2004.

Gibbons, Gail. **The Puffins Are Back**. HarperCollins, 1991.

Green, Jen. **Arctic Ocean**. World Almanac Library, 2006.

Kress, Stephen W. **Project Puffin: How We Brought Puffins Back to Egg Rock**. Tilbury House, 1997.

McMillan, Bruce. **Nights of the Pufflings**. Houghton Mifflin, 1995.

Tocci, Salvatore. **Arctic Tundra**. Franklin Watts, 2005.

**Organizations and Online Sites**

**Arctic Studies Center**
*http://www.mnh.si.edu/
arctic/html/puffin.html*

Check out this page about tufted puffins from the National Museum of Natural History of the Smithsonian Institution.

**Mainebirding**
*http://www.mainebirding.
net/puffin/*
Check out this site for detailed information about Atlantic puffins as well as information about those that live in Maine.

**NatureWorks**
*http://www.nhptv.org/
natureworks/hornedpuffin.htm*

This site from New Hampshire Public Television gives information about the characteristics, diet, habitat, and life cycle of the horned puffin.

**Project Puffin**
159 Sapsucker Woods Road
Ithaca, NY 14850
607-257-7308
*http://www.audubon.org/
bird/puffin/*

Project Puffin is a National Audubon Society program started in 1973. Its site includes lots of puffin photos, information, and links.

# Important Words

*burrows* holes in the ground where animals
live or nest

*colonies* large groups of animals that live
together

*decoys* fake birds that are made by humans
and used to attract real birds

*incubate* to hatch eggs by the warmth of
the body

*molt* to cast off an outer covering

*overfishing* fishing at a level that threatens
the survival of a kind of animal

*prey* an animal that is hunted and eaten by
other animals

*puffling* a puffin chick

*seabirds* birds that live and feed on the
open ocean

*species* a group of animals that have similar
characteristics and a common name

# Index

# Meet the Author

Ann O. Squire has a PhD in animal behavior. Before becoming a writer, she spent several years studying African electric fish and the special signals they use to communicate with each other. Dr. Squire is the author of many books on natural science and animals, including *Beluga Whales*, *Lemmings*, *Moose*, *Penguins*, and *Polar Bears*. She lives with her family in Katonah, New York.